Baby animals in northern forests

Bobbie Kalman
Crabtree Publishing Company
www.crabtreebooks.com

The Habitats of Baby Animals

Created by Bobbie Kalman

For Evangeline Siemens
You are a beautiful, brave girl.
Everyone sends you lots of love.

**Author and
Editor-in-Chief**
Bobbie Kalman

Editor
Kathy Middleton

Proofreader
Crystal Sikkens

Design
Bobbie Kalman
Katherine Berti
Samantha Crabtree
(front cover)

Photo research
Bobbie Kalman

Print and production coordinator
Katherine Berti

Photographs
Corel: p. 19 (top)
Dreamstime: p. 14 (bottom),
    24 (bottom left)
Thinkstock: back cover, p. 15 (top, bottom),
    18 (bottom)
All other images by Shutterstock

Library and Archives Canada Cataloguing in Publication

Kalman, Bobbie
    Baby animals in northern forests / Bobbie Kalman.

(The habitats of baby animals)
Includes index.
Issued also in electronic formats.
ISBN 978-0-7787-1018-9 (bound).--ISBN 978-0-7787-1031-8 (pbk.)

    1. Taiga animals--Infancy--Juvenile literature. 2. Taiga
ecology--Juvenile literature. I. Title. II. Series: Kalman, Bobbie.
Habitats of baby animals.

QL112.K3425 2013   j591.3'9209152   C2012-907720-8

Library of Congress Cataloging-in-Publication Data

CIP available at Library of Congress

Crabtree Publishing Company

www.crabtreebooks.com   1-800-387-7650

Printed in Canada/012013/MA20121217

**Published in Canada
Crabtree Publishing**
616 Welland Ave.
St. Catharines, Ontario
L2M 5V6

**Published in the United States
Crabtree Publishing**
PMB 59051
350 Fifth Avenue, 59th Floor
New York, New York 10118

**Published in the United Kingdom
Crabtree Publishing**
Maritime House
Basin Road North, Hove
BN41 1WR

**Published in Australia
Crabtree Publishing**
3 Charles Street
Coburg North
VIC, 3058

What is in this book?

What is a habitat?

A **habitat** is a place in nature. Plants and animals live in habitats. They are **living things**. Living things move, grow, change, and make new living things. Plants make new plants, and animals make babies.

This mother porcupine and her baby are living things. The trees and other plants around them are also living things.

What do living things need?

Habitats are made up of living and **non-living things**.

Air, sunshine, rocks, soil, and water are non-living things.

Living things need non-living things. They also need other living things. Living things find the things they need in their habitats.

What is a forest?

A forest is a habitat where many trees and other plants grow. Not all forests are the same. **Boreal forests** are in the northern areas of Earth. These forests also grow near mountaintops. Boreal forests have long winters and short summers.

This moose mother and her calves live in a boreal forest. Moose are the biggest kind of deer. They eat a lot of forest plants.

Northern forests

Most of the trees that grow in boreal forests are **conifers**. Conifers are **evergreen** trees with cones and sharp needle-like leaves. Evergreen trees do not lose their leaves in autumn.

cones

These black bear cubs have climbed up a tall conifer tree with their mother. Their thick fur coats protect them from the sharp needles of the tree.

Long, cold winters!

This young lynx has a thick fur coat to keep it warm in winter.

Winters are long and cold in boreal forests, and there is not much food for animals to eat. Some animals find small plants to eat under the snow at the edges of the forests. Others eat the tough leaves and cones of the conifers.

Sleep or migrate?

Some animals **migrate**, or move, to warmer areas for the winter. Others go into a deep sleep. Squirrels sleep soundly during winter, but they do get up now and then to look for food. Bears spend most of the winter in a deep sleep.

These deer cannot find plants to eat, so they eat the tough bark of a conifer tree.

This young red fox is looking for rabbits that may be hiding under the snow in the forest.

Brown bears sleep through most of winter, but these cubs woke up to drink milk from their sleepy mother.

Forest homes

Many animals make homes in their forest habitat. Some mothers keep their babies safe in nests high up in trees. Others find **dens**, or homes, under rocks or inside hollow logs. Wolf pups, for example, stay in their dens for their first month of life. Their mother then allows them to go outside.

This mother wolf and one of her pups have fallen asleep in their den. Mother wolves stay with their pups for the first three weeks to keep them safe.

These great gray owlets live in a nest near the top of an evergreen tree. To practice flying, the owlets jump from branch to branch.

This **fawn**, or baby deer, does not live in a nest or den. It hides among the plants on the forest floor.

Boreal forest babies

These are a few of the baby animals that live in boreal forests. They include deer, moose, lynx, squirrels, wolves, cougars, porcupines, black bears, and brown bears.

deer
fawn

black
bear cub

brown
bear cubs

porcupine pup or porcupette

What are mammals?

The animals on these pages are **mammals**. Mammals have hair or fur. How do mammals move? Name three ways.

gray wolf
pup

*lynx
kitten*

*cougar
cub*

*red squirrel
pup*

*moose
calf*

Mothers and babies

Mammal mothers feed their babies and teach them how to find their own food. After they are born, the babies drink milk made in the bodies of their mothers. Drinking mother's milk is called **nursing**. Some mammal babies nurse for several months, or even years.

Wolf pups nurse until they are eight to ten weeks old. They then start eating meat that their mother brings up from her stomach.

Taking care

Mothers take good care of their young and keep them safe. They hide them from predators and teach them how to hunt or find plants to eat. The babies need to learn how to stay alive in their boreal forest habitat.

This mother lynx will look after her kitten for about one year.

Plant eaters

pine seeds

Bison eat mainly grasses and small plants that grow close to the ground. This bison family is grazing at the edge of a boreal forest.

Animals eat different kinds of foods. Some eat plants. Animals that eat mainly plants are called **herbivores**. Not all herbivores eat the same kinds of plants, or even the same parts of plants. **Grazers** are herbivores that eat mainly grasses. Other herbivores eat leaves, twigs, fruit, nuts, or pine seeds.

Browsing for food

Many herbivores eat the leaves of plants. Herbivores that eat leaves are called **browsers**. Browsers eat the leaves of bushes and small trees. When there are no leaves to eat, they eat tree bark.

In summer, this young porcupine eats twigs, roots, stems, and berries. In winter, it eats conifer needles and tree bark.

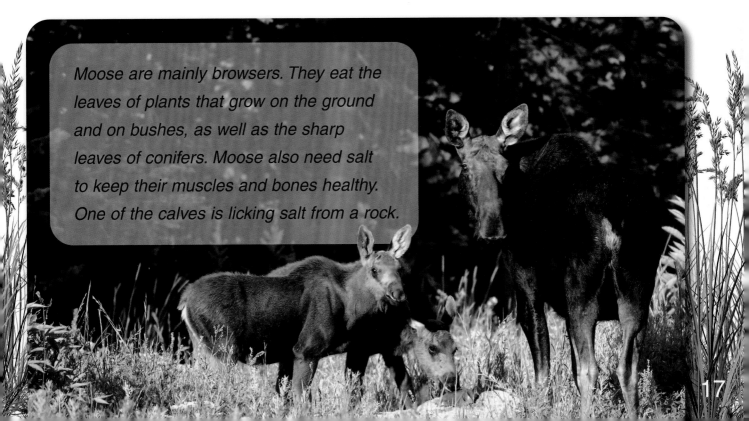

Moose are mainly browsers. They eat the leaves of plants that grow on the ground and on bushes, as well as the sharp leaves of conifers. Moose also need salt to keep their muscles and bones healthy. One of the calves is licking salt from a rock.

Baby carnivores

Carnivores are animals that eat other animals. Lynx, cougars, and wolves are carnivores that live in boreal forests. Most carnivores are also predators. The animals they hunt are called **prey**. Predator babies start learning how to hunt weeks or months after they are born.

snowshoe hare

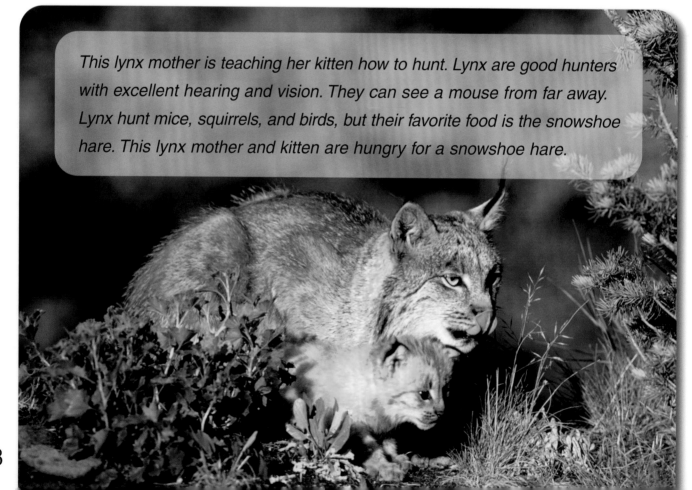

This lynx mother is teaching her kitten how to hunt. Lynx are good hunters with excellent hearing and vision. They can see a mouse from far away. Lynx hunt mice, squirrels, and birds, but their favorite food is the snowshoe hare. This lynx mother and kitten are hungry for a snowshoe hare.

Cougars hunt deer, sheep, wild pigs, and even elk and moose. This cougar cub looks for a squirrel to eat. It leaps on its prey when it hunts.

At the age of two months, wolf pups go on hunting trips with adult wolves to watch how they hunt. At eight months, the young wolves are big enough to join the hunt.

Baby omnivores

Omnivores are animals that eat both plants and other animals. They can find food more easily than herbivores or carnivores can because they eat more than one kind of food. Boreal forest omnivores include brown bears, black bears, and red squirrels. Most omnivores have a much better chance of staying alive because they eat any food they can find.

These brown bear cubs are omnivores. They eat nuts, berries, grasses, flowers, and roots. They also eat honey, as well as the bees that make it! Brown bears eat fish, mice, and rabbits, too. They also eat foods that other animals or people leave behind.

Eurasian
red squirrel

North American
red squirrel

Red squirrels make nests in evergreen trees, where they can find plenty of pine cones. In winter, they eat the seeds of 40 to 50 cones a day. During the summer, red squirrels eat nuts, berries, flowers, and insects. They also eat bird eggs and even some baby animals, like mice, rabbits, and **leverets**, or baby hares.

A forest food chain

sun

energy

All living things need **energy**. Without energy, living things cannot move or grow. Energy starts with the sun. Plants use the sun's energy to make food. Animals get their energy by eating plants or other animals. Each time they eat, the sun's energy gets passed along to them. The passing of energy from one living thing to another is called a **food chain**. Follow the arrows and numbers to see how the energy flows from the sun, to plants, to animals.

1. Plants make food from sunlight. The sun's energy goes into the plants.

energy

energy

3. When a lynx kitten eats a squirrel, the sun's energy is passed along from the plants to the squirrel and then to the kitten.

2. When a squirrel eats a plant, the sun's energy is passed along to the squirrel.

23

Words to know and Index

babies
pages 4, 10,
11, 12–13,
14–15, 18, 21

food
pages 8, 9,
14, 15, 16–17,
18–19, 20–21,
22–23

food chain
pages
22–23

forests (trees)
pages 4, 6–7, 8,
9, 10, 11, 12,
15, 16, 17, 18,
20, 21, 22

habitats (homes)
pages 4–5, 6, 10–11, 15

mammals
pages 13,
14, 15

Other index words
carnivores pages 18–19, 20
conifers pages 7, 8, 9, 17
herbivores pages 16–17, 20
living things pages 4, 5, 22
migration page 8
non-living things page 5
nursing page 14
omnivores pages 20–21
plants pages 4, 6, 8, 9, 11,
     15, 16–17, 20, 22, 23
predators pages 15, 18
sleep pages 8, 9

mothers
pages 4, 6, 7, 9,
10, 14–15, 18

winter
pages 6,
8–9, 21